Cambridge Early Years

Communication and Language

for English as a First Language

Learner's Book 2B

Gill Budgell

Contents

Note to parents and practitioners   3

Block 3: Working and playing together   4

Block 4: Wonderful water   18

Acknowledgements   32

Note to parents and practitioners

This Learner's Book provides activities to support the second term of FLE Communication and Language for Cambridge Early Years 2.

Activities can be used at school or at home. Children will need support from an adult. Additional guidance about activities can be found in the **For practitioners** boxes.

Stories are provided for children to enjoy looking at and listening to. Children are not expected to be able to read the stories themselves.

Children will encounter the following characters within this book. You could ask children to point to the characters when they see them on the pages, and say their names.

The Learner's Book activities support the Teaching Resource activities. The Teaching Resource provides step-by-step coverage of the Cambridge Early Years curriculum and guidance on how the Learner's Book activities develop the curriculum learning statements.

Hi, my name is Mia.

Find us on the front covers doing lots of fun activities.

Hi, my name is Gemi.

Hi, my name is Rafi.

Hi, my name is Kiho.

Block 3

Working and playing together

A Gift for Amma: Market Day in India

by Meera Sriram

The sun grows bright. The street is busy. It's market day in town!

I count my money and dash outside to find a treasure for Amma.

SAFFRON orange strands in tiny scoops. Would Amma like to season rice?

Orange marigolds swing over doors – *swish, swish!* Should I make her a garland?

JASMINE white in starry blooms, petals to perfume Amma's braid.

But white goats shove past – *shoo, shoo!* I squirm away.

LOTUS pink shimmering fresh. Would Amma like dewy buds?

Pink sweets soaked in ghee – *yum, yum!* I'll come back for my treat.

PEACOCK green dancing in the breeze ... would she need a fan for the heat?

Green herbs – mint and coriander – *sniff, sniff!* I'm hungry for chutney.

VERMILION red like rising flame, but Amma never dots her forehead.

Red-hot peppers spill over – *achoo, achoo!* I cover my face.

CHARCOAL black fires up fast,
ready to roast sweetcorn and kebabs.

Black drums beat and boom –
hop, skip! What would Amma like?

TURMERIC yellow like sunshine dust,
plenty of powdery spice at home.

A yellow rickshaw pedals by –
ding-a-ling! I scoot to the side.

PIGEON grey at every corner, street birds pecking grains.

Grey buffalo blinks and stomps – *moo, moo!* I must hurry.

TERRACOTTA brown baked from clay, cool water in delicate pots.

Brown tea with milk and sugar – *"Tea, tea!"* I smell cardamom.

… a gift just for Amma!

My favourite colours

Draw and write.

Choose 4 colours from the story.
Draw something that is the same colour. Label it.

For practitioners

Encourage children to choose 4 colours from the story *A Gift for Amma*. In each box, ask them to draw and label something that is the same colour as one of their chosen colours. Prompt talk using the language from the text about things that they like or that are the same colour.

Story bag

Choose and say.

Draw lines to add some things to your story bag. Talk about the things you choose.

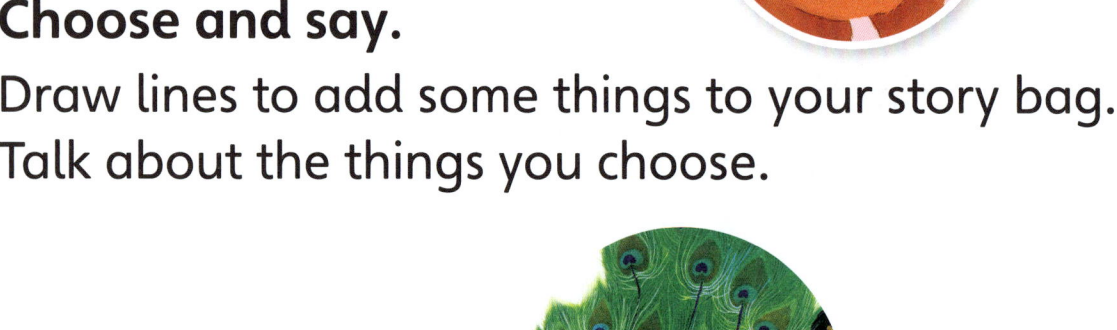

For practitioners

Encourage children to reflect on the story, *A Gift for Amma*, and to select some of the things to include in their story bag. They may use their choices to talk about the story or to retell it.

A gift for Amma

Think and draw.

What gift would you choose for Amma or a friend? Draw the gift.

For practitioners
Ask children to think about what gift they would give to Amma or their friend. They draw their gift in the frame. Some children may like to have a caption scribed or try to write one themselves.

Chocolate Milkshake by Tania Mead

Into the blender …
CHOCOLATE!
1 spoon, 2 spoon,
3 spoon
What the heck
4 spoon, 5 spoon

Now the milk
GLUG …
GLUG …
SLURP

Scoop in the
ice-cream –
PLOP … PLOP …

Turn the switch
SHAKE ... SHAKE ... SLURP ...

GURGLE ... GURGLE ...

Pour into glass

GLUG ... GLUG ...

Ahh

Chocolate milkshake

Join the dots.

Talk about what goes in the blender to make a chocolate milkshake.

For practitioners

Children join the dots and say the instructions like the poem. Some may almost be reciting the poem, whilst others may describe the pictures as instructions. Remind children of the differences between a poem and a recipe text.

What you need to make a chocolate milkshake

Colour and say.

For practitioners
Encourage children to talk about what they would need to make a chocolate milkshake. Show or remind them of the recipe, and invite them to colour in the ingredients (*chocolate powder, milk, ice cream*) and the utensils (*glass, jug, blender, scoop*).

Block 4 Wonderful water

An underwater curiosity box

Think and draw.

What would you put in an underwater curiosity box? Draw in the box.

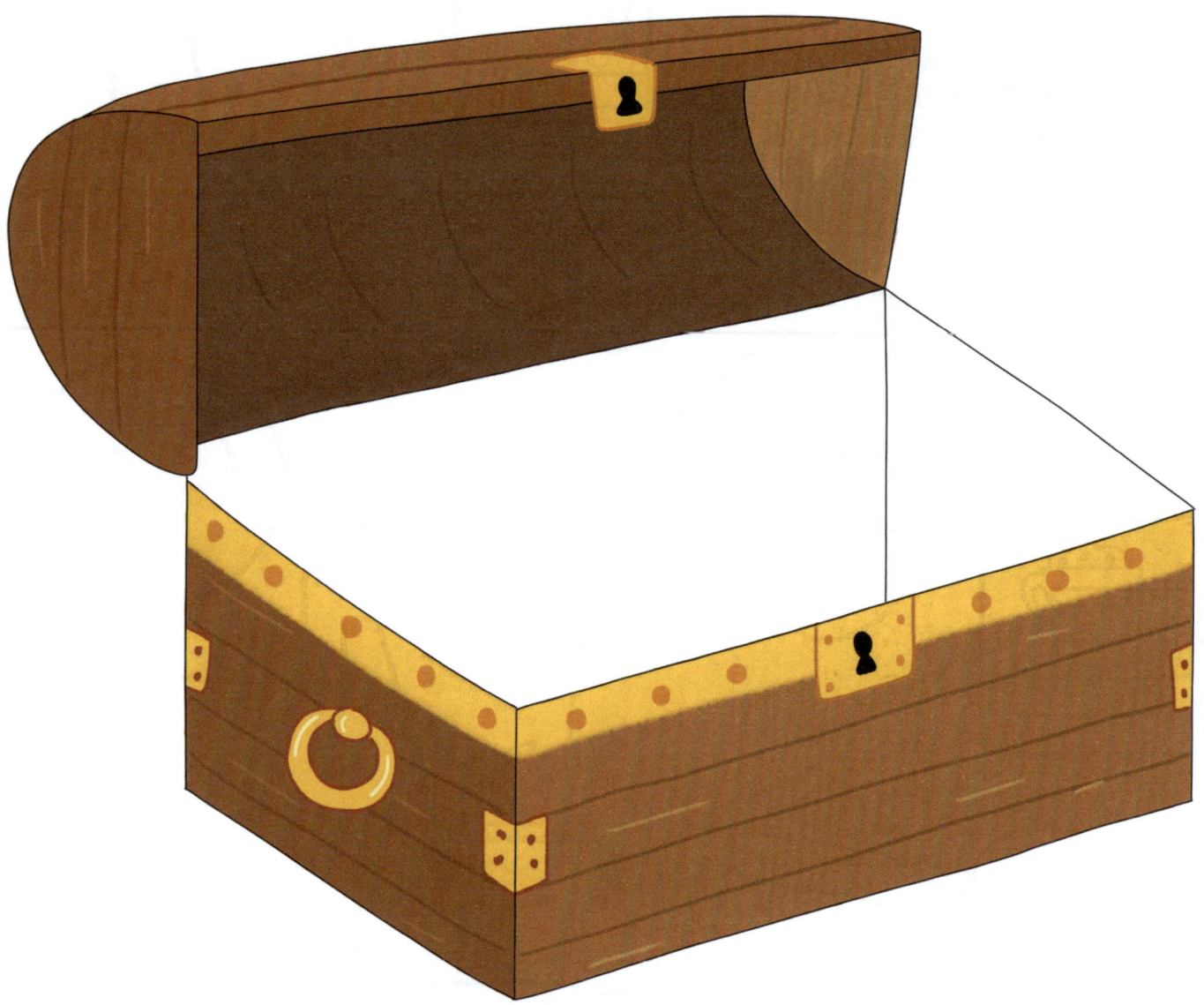

For practitioners

Children draw items to go in their own underwater curiosity box and attempt to talk about or write what is in it.

Surprising Sharks by Nicola Davies

You're swimming in the warm blue sea. What's the one word that turns your dream into a nightmare?

What's the one word that makes you think of a giant man-eating KILLER?

SHAAAAARRRKK!

Shark? Yes, it is a shark!

It's a **DWARF LANTERN SHARK**. It's the smallest kind of shark in the world, just bigger than a chocolate bar. Not a giant, certainly no man-eater and a killer only if you happen to be a shrimp.

You see, MOST sharks are not at all what you might expect. After all, who would expect a shark to ...

Like all lantern sharks this **BLACKBELLY LANTERN SHARK** can make light shine from its tummy. This helps it to blend in with the silvery surface of the sea and avoid ending up as dinner for bigger fish.

have built-in fairy lights ...

or blow up like a party balloon ...

SWELL SHARKS swallow water when they get scared and blow up to three times their normal size so that they can wedge themselves between rocks and no predator can pull them out.

In fact, sharks come in all sorts of shapes and sizes.

BLUE SHARK

COOKIE-CUTTER SHARK

NURSE SHARK

ANGEL SHARK

GOBLIN SHARK

How can such different animals all be sharks? Look carefully and you'll see all the things they share.

TAIL

DORSAL FIN

PELVIC FIN

PECTORAL FIN

Fins and tails for swimming ...
A shark's tail fins are bigger at the top than at the bottom, unlike other fish's tails. Their tails push them through the water and the fins help them to swim left or right, up or down.

Outside:

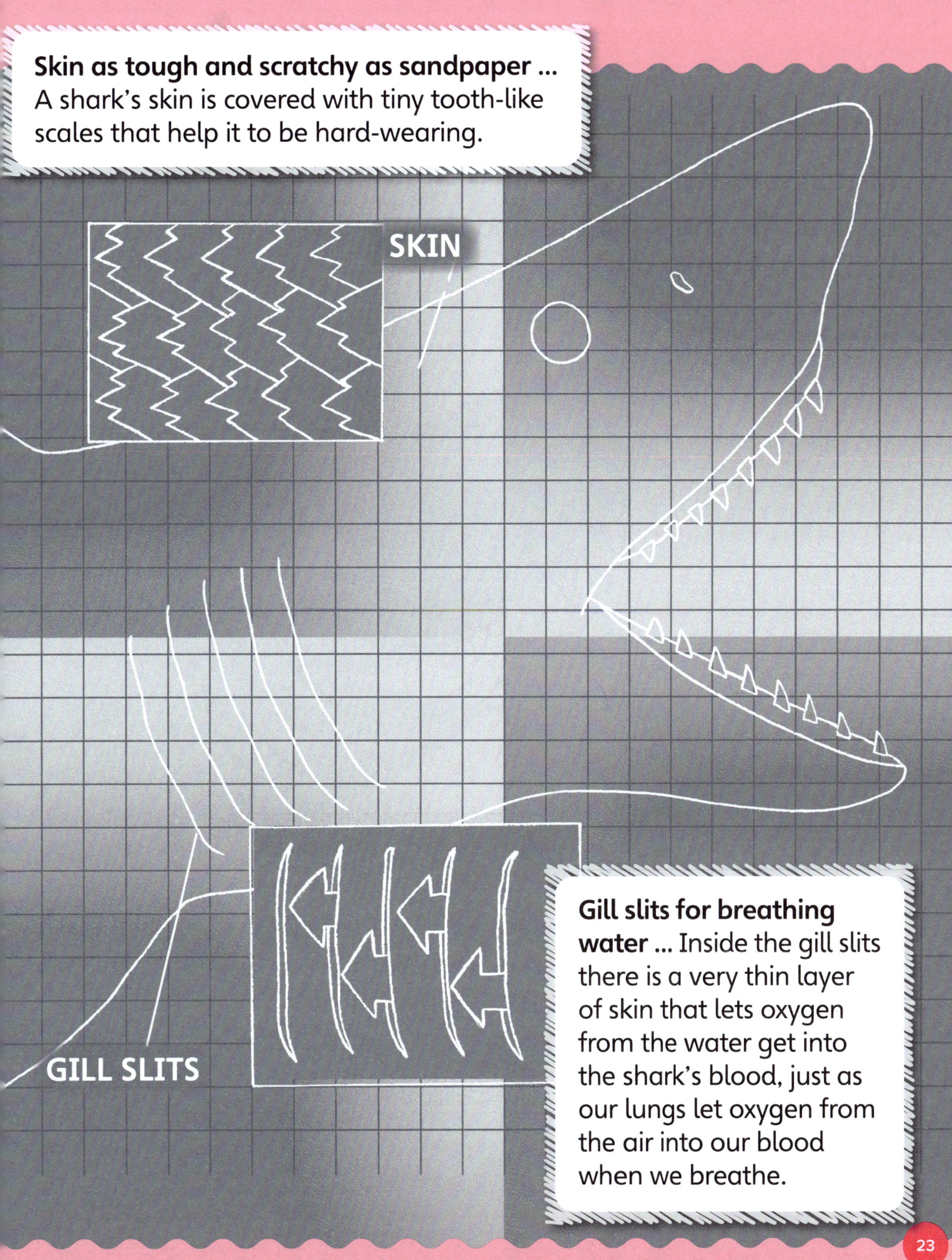

Skin as tough and scratchy as sandpaper ...
A shark's skin is covered with tiny tooth-like scales that help it to be hard-wearing.

SKIN

GILL SLITS

Gill slits for breathing water ... Inside the gill slits there is a very thin layer of skin that lets oxygen from the water get into the shark's blood, just as our lungs let oxygen from the air into our blood when we breathe.

Shark features

Match and write.

Look at the shark picture and the words. Label the shark.

For practitioners
Talk to the children about the shark drawing and the label lines. Explain that they should label the shark. Help them to find the right words from the box and ask them to copy them into the correct places to match the story picture.

tail
fin
skin
gills
teeth

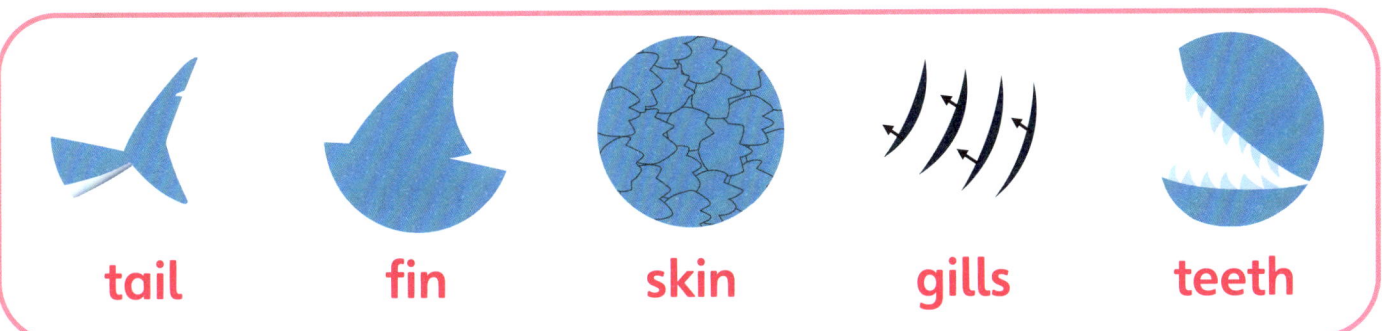

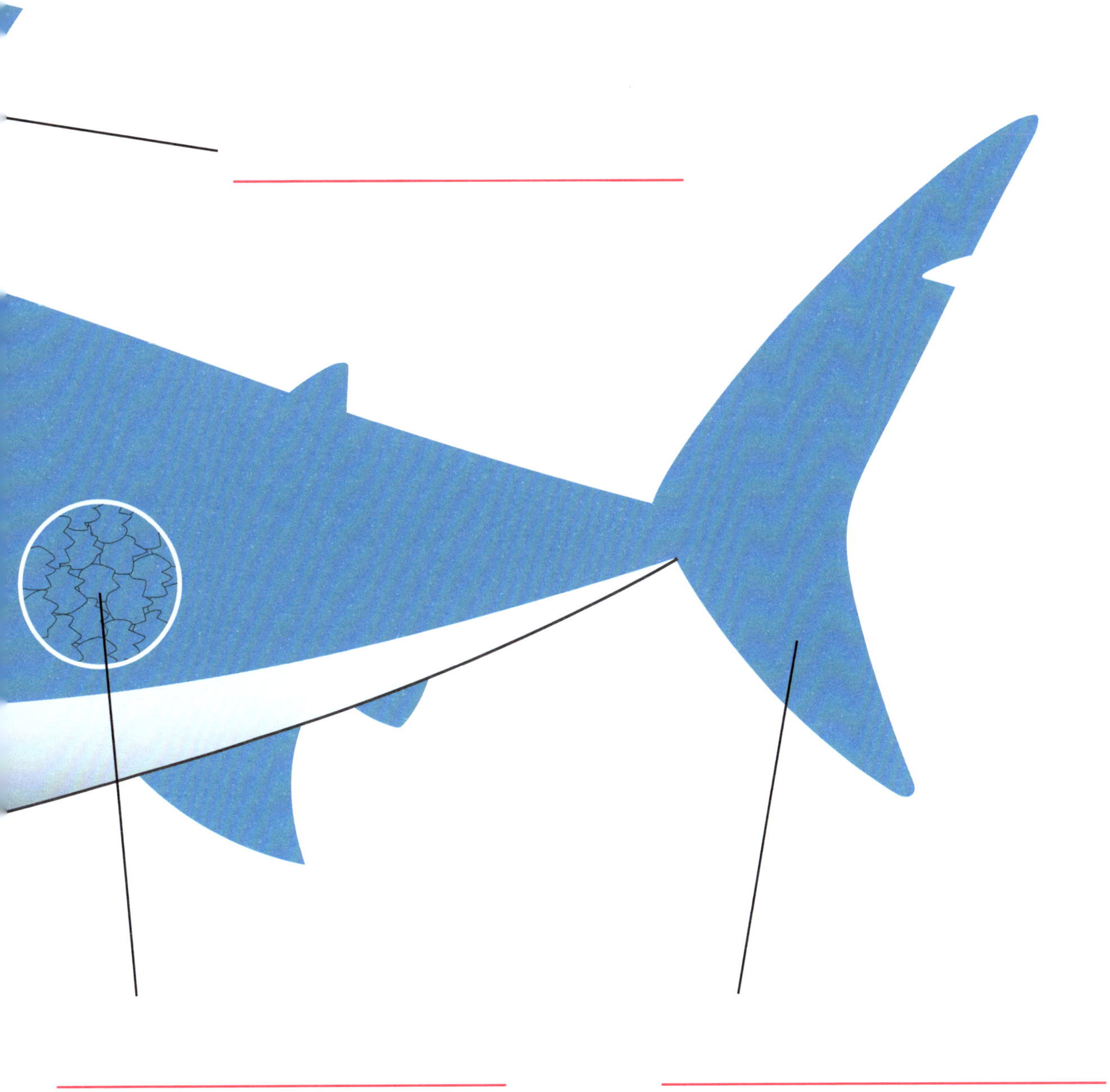

My favourite shark

Think and write.

Draw your favourite shark and write its name.

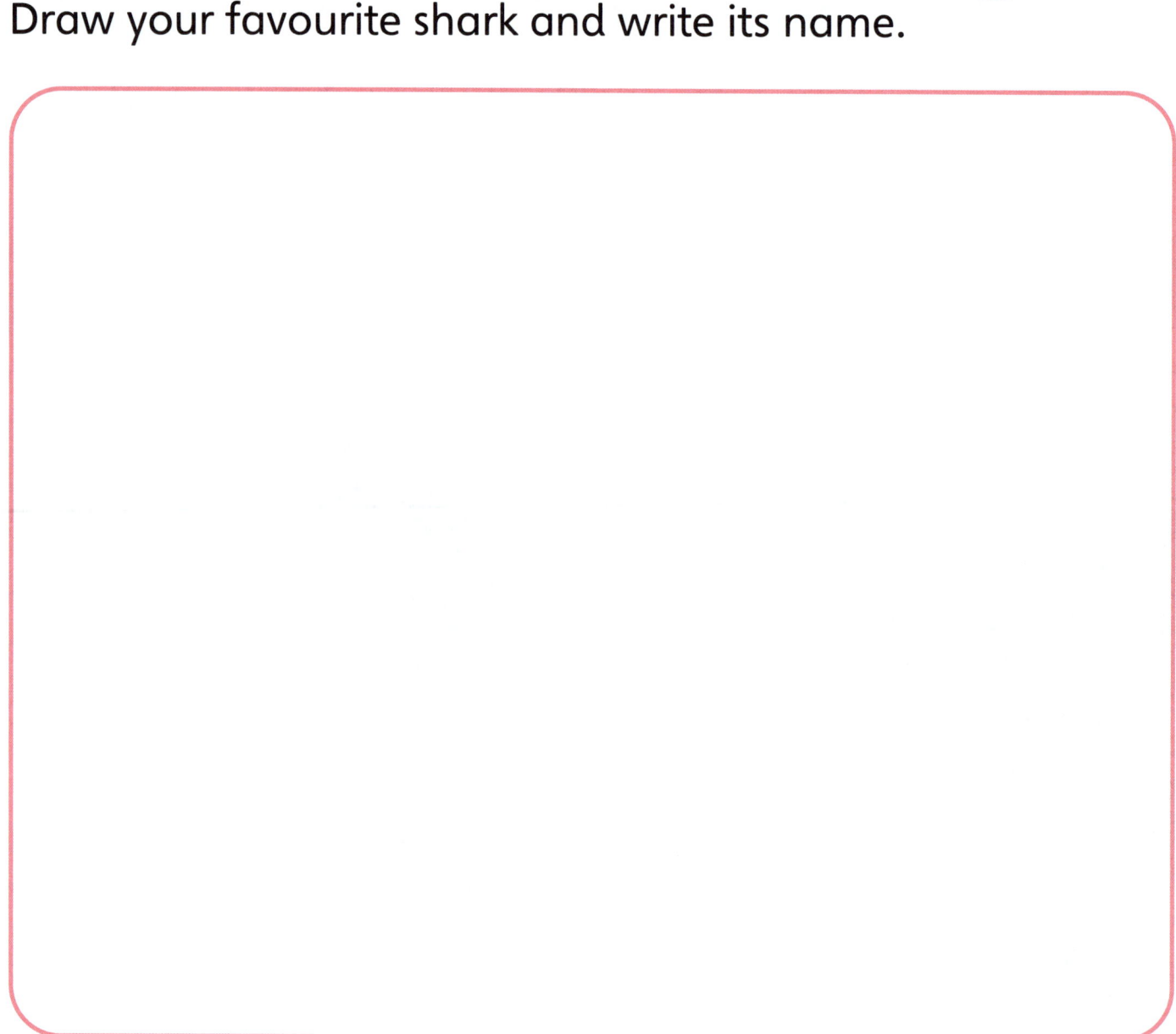

My favourite shark is _____ .

For practitioners

Encourage children to say which is their favourite shark from the text or from others they know. They draw it with some attention to detail and using the language of the text, before writing its name carefully. Support children as necessary with names to copy.

Here is the Ostrich (Anonymous)

Here is the ostrich, straight and tall,
(Raise arm, fingers drooping.)
Nodding his head above us all.

Here is the long snake on the ground,
(Wiggle hand and arm.)
Wriggling on the stones he found.

Here are the eagles that fly so high,
(Flap arms.)
Spreading their wings across the sky.

Here is the hedgehog, prickly and small,
(Wrap hands into a ball.)
Rolling himself into a ball.

Here is the spider scuttling around,
(Walk fingers like spider.)
Treading so lightly on the ground.

Here are the children fast asleep,
(Rest head on hands clasped palm to palm.)

And here are the owls excited to peep!
(Make thumb and fingers into spectacles around eyes, move head side to side.)

Here is the ...

Listen and tick ✓.

Listen for the animals mentioned in the rhyme.

For practitioners

Read the poem aloud to the children. Ask them to find and tick the picture of each animal when they hear it in the rhyme.

Action!

Match and say.

Match the animal or person to the correct action. Name them.

For practitioners
Children draw a line to match the animal or person to the correct action from the rhyme. Encourage them to say their names, e.g., *ostrich, snake, bird, hedgehog, spider, child, owl* and to again practise making the actions.

Acknowledgements

The authors and publishers acknowledge the following sources of copyright material and are grateful for the permissions granted. While every effort has been made, it has not always been possible to identify the sources of all the material used, or to trace all copyright holders. If any omissions are brought to our notice, we will be happy to include the appropriate acknowledgements on reprinting.

A Gift for Amma: Market Day in India Text copyright © 2020 by Meera Sriram. Illustrations copyright © 2020 by Mariona Cabassa. Used with permission from Barefoot Books, Ltd.

'Chocolate Milkshake' by Tania Mead originally in *Take a Chance: An Anthology of Performance Poetry*, Australian Association of Teachers, 1981

Extract from SURPRISING SHARKS Written by Nicola Davies & Illustrated by James Croft. Text © 2003 Nicola Davies, Illustrations © 2003 James Croft. Reproduced by permission of Walker Books Ltd, London SW11 5HJ

Thanks to the following artists at Beehive Illustration:

Tamara Joubert, Michelle McGovern, Sarah Pitt, Sara Ramos.

Cover characters by Becky Davies (The Bright Agency)